Echos of the Heart

Amanda Davis

BookLeaf Publishing

India | USA | UK

Presentation by *BookLeaf Publishing*

Web: www.bookleafpub.com

E-mail: info@bookleafpub.com

ISBN: 9789367392119

First edition 2024

To my husband,

From the very beginning, you've always believed in me—when I couldn't see it myself. Your love, encouragement, and unwavering faith in my dreams have been the foundation of everything I do. This book is as much yours as it is mine, and it's because of you that I've found the courage to share my heart with the world.

ACKNOWLEDGEMENT

I am deeply grateful for the love and support I have received from those closest to me. To my mom and grandma, your wisdom, encouragement, and faith in me have been a constant source of strength. To my dad, though you are no longer with us, your presence continues to guide me. Your belief in me still echoes in my heart, and I carry your love with me every day.

To my husband, thank you for being my rock and my greatest inspiration—your unwavering support makes everything possible. I'm also grateful for the prayers, love, and encouragement of my church community, and for my inner circle of friends whose loyalty and understanding have kept me grounded.

This book is a reflection of all the love, faith, and strength I have received from each of you, and I carry that with me as I share it with the world.

PREFACE

Echos of the Heart is a deeply personal collection of poems, shaped by the moments that connect us, break us, and ultimately help us heal. Each verse reflects the quiet power of love, the weight of loss, and the resilience that carries us through. This book is an exploration of how the heart endures, both in the joy of new beginnings and the sorrow of goodbyes. My hope is that these poems speak to you as they have to me—reminding us that even in our most vulnerable moments, we are united by the echoes of our shared experiences.

Echos of the Heart

When a woman knows what she wants, it
sets a fire under her,
So she can keep pushing toward the goal
And get what's waiting for her.
It's happiness she deserves,
Because she's always setting others up,
Making her own happiness somewhat stuck
in a rut.
The happiness she sees in other people,
That she's known her whole existence,
They are the goal.
She'll have it too,
And it will make her new,
Again. It will make her whole.

The happiness that's provided by loyalty,
companionship,
Adoration, and acceptance,
That's not without being guided by the One.
He knows where my future lies.

It's only natural to want time to speed up.
Happiness knows no limits
And will not tell you, "Enough is enough."
It's time and patience with life's embrace
And future's kisses.

The goal of happiness, of what one
wishes—
She will find it,
This much is true.
She will find it within herself,
And her heart will know it too.

In the echos of the heart,
The happiness awaits.
After all, with God, her love, her family, and
time,
It's never too late.

Amore Mio (Sonetto)

This man's brown eyes, I could swim in forever,
I could get lost, but not in fear or doubt.
It's easy to say that I'll leave—never,
While my feelings linger strong, without a doubt.

He is a safe haven for me, you see,
I've never seen it quite this way before.
Anywhere I go, he'll always be,
My love, my partner, and so much more.

That is why he was sent just for me here—
Everything feels perfect; he makes it clear.

Listen to it Echo

Don't overcompensate for what they lack
inside.
At the end of the day,
have some sense and change back tonight.
And when in doubt, find a way.
All these extra feelings over simple things—
it's not your job to please these human
beings.

They're the ice, you're the fire,
cold-hearted… they have no desire
to better themselves or even go higher
than the level they've reached.
It's nothing to admire.
If you listen, I will teach you how to
trust and believe that you can do it.
There's nothing more to wait for—just tell
yourself you'll get through it.

You'll find comfort in your peace when you
cut negativity off.
You owe it to yourself to tell them enough is
enough.
Listen to it echo. LISTEN to it echo…
LISTEN. That's your heart.

Until the end of time- my favorite thing

Seasons change, but you stay the same, I am so glad you're mine.

You've shown me how it feels to be loved, how it feels to shine.

You look in my eyes like I'm everything, like I'm you're where when and why

I'll love you always, I'll love you still,
Always, forever, until the end of time.
✰✰✰

You···

My favorite hug,

My favorite kiss,

My favorite night,

My favorite miss,

My favorite feeling,

My favorite forever,

My favorite, favorite thing.

I do

I find comfort in the changes, as long as I am with you.
Nothing seems impossible with our future in view.
The next step, this journey, the rest of our days—
Is the perfection I've always dreamed of.
It's just right in all the ways.

I am content with the joining of our hearts and our last
names.
The best day ever, my love,
Means life will never be the same—
Only better, moving forward, and always for the good.

In love with you, I said "I do," forever, understood.

For you, Uncle

For You, Uncle

It was unexpected
When we got the call that day—
You had taken your last breath,
And then you slipped away.

You were gone in just a blink;
We thought you were doing fine.
But just like that, upstairs you went—
You were next in line.

If I could pick up the phone
And hear your voice again,
You'd say, "We're going fishing,"
And tell me where and when.

You taught me how to do so much:
How to bait a hook,
How to sit atop a surfboard
And take a far-off look.

If I could just go back in time
To spend more days with you,
I'd call, I'd text, I'd drive—
Whatever I could do.

For now, I'll say, "Happy Birthday"
From all of us this year.
We'll light a candle in your honor
And play your songs down here.

To celebrate and remember
One of the best men I ever knew—
For you, Uncle, I wrote it down.
This one is for you.

I can love you from here

I Can Love You From Here

I know I said it wasn't fair
When you told me I wasn't it for you.
But now that we've grown so close,
I can't see a future without the view of you.

It all happened so fast—
A spark of light from your past.
And I told you through all of the tears:
I'll still be your best friend
Until the very end.
Just know,
I can love you from here.

You told me that you got engaged,
And I told you I was happy for you.
You asked me to speak that day
About the future that was right in front of
you.

It all happened so fast—
A spark of light from your past,
A mixture of emotional tears.
I am still your best friend;

My promise will never end.
Just know,
I can love you from here.

You often apologize
For the way things happened to go.
It's nobody's fault.
You love who you love, I know…

It all happened so fast—
A spark of light from your past,
Nothing more than happy tears.
I am still your best friend;
I promise, until the very end.
Just know,
I can love you from here.

I'm okay—
I hope you know.

I can love you… from here.

He follows in front

He Follows in Front

He follows in front,
From the other side, you see.
He lingers a bit.

I can't hide from him,
His blade swings, every time.
He's coming, I see.

All my fear and doubt,
It's mostly wonder, about
Why is he still there?

Lacking body rest,
My thoughts are torn asunder,
Inconceivable.

Driving, in my sleep,
He appears before my eyes,
Swinging it once more.

What does this mean, now?
It is not my time to go.
Can you tell me what—

Vanishing, again.
Demise, inevitable.
That is not his goal.

He stays, not away.
He leaves, then He reappears.
He follows in front.

Demise? No, my friend.
A chapter will simply end,
Life transitioning.

It's not a sunset,
But a brand-new dawn breaking,
A new horizon.

Unavoidable,
He follows in front, again…
But, now I know why.

Rhythmic Symphony of the Heart

Heartbeats, like whispers in the night,
Pulse with life's electric might.
They speak of love, of fears untold,
Of dreams that soar and hearts that hold.

With their rhythms strong, they dance and play,
Echoing the highs and lows of the day.
With every thump, a tale is spun—
Of battles fought and victories won.

They drum the beat of endless chase,
Of passions wild, of tender embrace.
In syncopated beats, they find their groove,
A modern symphony of life, they prove.

So listen close to each other's heartbeat's call,
For in their rhythm, we find it all—
The joy, the pain, the hopes we keep,
In every pulsing, rhythmic leap.

Shoreline

On the shoreline of tomorrow,
I hope you'll find,
That a new beginning is coming,
With the best view of you in mind.
No matter what comes,
I'll never leave your side—
The wind to my water,
The sand to my tide.

Each wave will carry whispers,
Of stories yet untold,
And every grain of sand beneath,
Will shimmer like pure gold.

The breeze will hum with promise,
The skies will softly glow,
Guiding your steps forward,
To places you've yet to know.
On the shoreline of tomorrow,
Let hope and courage bind,
For a new beginning is coming,
With the best view of you in mind.

Forever Changed

You didn't lose her when you left her behind.
She is always there, always in the back of
your mind.
It is yours, after all, so you can never fall out
of line—
you only find new avenues because they're
there to find.

You want what's best for you,
what's best for your heart this time.
You can't live in the past,
even though it's where you hide.

Deep inside, in the corners of your mind,
lies the piece of your past you fear to find—
the one you thought you left behind.

But you always have a way to run,
a way to get away.
The past is behind you,
and the future is right in front of your face.

Your heart is secure now,
held by the one who saved it.
Through the fight of faith and union,
you are forever changed.

You have the heart and the courage
to move forward with your days.
You don't have to live in the shadows of
your progress—
it's okay to go at your own pace.

So, come on, girl—
seize the day.

It's yours.
There's nothing left to say.

Eternal

You
Make me
Feel like me
You make me complete
This is the best feeling
I never want to let go
Now that I have the chance to
Keep you forever

And I will always
Be your love
Forever more
Yours

Birthday Song

Today is mine, a day of cheer,
Yet I feel the weight of another year.
The laughter fades, a quiet song,
For the one I miss, who's been gone so
long.

No phone call comes, no melody rings,
No voice to hum the song you'd sing.
I close my eyes, and there you are,
A whispered wish, a guiding star.

I celebrate still, with love all around,
But your absence lingers, a hollow sound.
Dad, I miss you—your warmth, your grace,
Today and always, no one takes your place.

Missing You on this Day

I miss your cooking on Thanksgiving Day,
The prayers you'd offer as we bowed to
pray.
You spoke of family, love, and grace,
A warmth no time or space could replace.

I miss the hugs you gave so tight,
The way you made the world feel right.
And how you'd marvel, with joy so small,
At the beauty of the leaves in fall.

Then came December, with its festive cheer,
Prepping for Christmas we held so dear.
You'd find the perfect tree, so tall, so grand,
Decorating together, hand in hand.

We sang the songs, old and new,
And watched the movies, our favorite few.
Visits to family, laughter and care,
Moments of magic we'd always share.

Your presence lingers, soft and near,
In every laugh, in every tear.
Though you're not here, your love remains,
A part of us in joy and pain.

You Never Let Me Down

You make me feel like I can fly,
A soaring heart, never let down.
Forever lifted, reaching high,
Feet far from the trembling ground.

Adventure waits, the path is clear,
You guide me through the winding way.
The past may linger, but no fear—
We greet the dawn, a brand-new day.

Free falling, yet you're always there,
A steady hand, a loving light.
Through shadows past, the future's fair,
With you, my world is pure and bright.

Things are looking up, I see,
The clouds are gone, the sun breaks free.
Together, bound, yet still unchained,
A life rebuilt, a love reclaimed.

You never let me down, my guide,
Through every storm, you're by my side.

You Never Let Me Down (Song Edition)

(Verse 1)
You make me feel like I can fly,
You never let me down.
My heart is forever whole and lifted,
All the way off the ground.

(Pre-Chorus)
It's the best way I've found,
To feel free, to say I've found my way up.
You never let me down.

(Chorus)
Free fallin', but you catch me always,
You never let me down.
When the sky turns gray, you bring the sun,
You never let me down.

(Verse 2)
My future adventure awaits,
You know how to lead the way.
Through the shadows of my past,
I never thought I'd see the day.

(Pre-Chorus)

Where you and I could take a chance,
Appreciate the past, but walk away.
It's fine for it to stay where it lives,
And welcome a brighter day.

(Chorus)
Free fallin', but you catch me always,
You never let me down.
When the sky turns gray, you bring the sun,
You never let me down.

(Bridge)
Things are looking up, I say,
We're flying higher every day.
Let the past fade far behind,
Your hand in mine, we redefine.

(Whispers) Its our time.

(Chorus)
Free fallin', but you catch me always,
You never let me down.
When the sky turns gray, you bring the sun,
You never let me down.

(Outro)
It's the best way I've found,
To feel free, to say I've found my way up.

You never let me down.

Whispers

Little notes of quiet voices,
Echoes of silent thoughts—
On and on,
All around me,
And within.

A quiet sound of negative noise,
The hum of words unspoken.
Lack of emphasized volume,
Yet loud enough to feel.

Whispers,
Soft and fleeting,
Yet lingering,
Filling the spaces
Between the silence.

Made for me

In my zone,
I stand alone,
Chasing dreams that call to me.
A vision clear,
Beyond the fear,
Of what the future holds to see.

No doubt remains,
Through joy or pain,
A truth my heart could always see:
I'm incomplete,
Until I meet,
The partner that was made for me.

Through silent nights,
And endless fights,
I've learned the value of the wait.
For what is love,
If not the gift,
Of finding someone marked by fate?

Made for me (Song Edition)

Verse 1
In my zone, I stand alone,
Chasing dreams I've yet to see.
Through the dark, I spark a flame,
Burning for what's meant to be.

Pre-Chorus
No doubt inside, I feel it strong,
A love that's waited all along.

Chorus
I can't live without, I know it's true,
The missing piece of me is you.
Through every trial, you'll set me free,
My partner, you were made for me.

Verse 2
Through the storms and silent nights,
I've held onto this belief.
What is love but patient faith,
The kind that brings your soul relief?

Pre-Chorus
No doubt inside, I feel it strong,
A love that's waited all along.

Chorus

I can't live without, I know it's true,
The missing piece of me is you.
Through every trial, you'll set me free,
My partner, you were made for me.

Bridge
Every tear, every fight,
Led me closer to the light.
Now I see, it's destiny,
You were always meant for me.

Chorus
I can't live without, I know it's true,
The missing piece of me is you.
Through every trial, you'll set me free,
My partner, you were made for me.

Outro
In my zone, I'm not alone,
You're the dream I longed to see.
No doubt remains, love's here to stay,
My partner, you were made for me.

Everlasting Evermore

The way I feel about you
Gets stronger
The more I see out of you
Creates an overflow of attraction
To the very being that IS you
You're the only next person I could ever want
To see with me forever
My everlasting evermore

Until you

I'm not used to this,
This level of admiration,
This level of perfection.

My whole life, I watched,
Dad treated Mom like a queen,
Mom treated Dad like a king—
Even before the ring.

But my adult years have shown,
I've been the jester, a joke,
Something to toy with, to break.

I told myself it's the times,
This generation's cruel design.
I thought I'd never know
What "top of the line" could feel like—
Until you.

Go ahead, break my shell,
Tear down that wall.
I think I can give in to it,
I think I'll let myself fall.